Landmark
insights.
Book 2

Redefine What's Possible

Landmark®

Published by
Landmark Worldwide
353 Sacramento St., Ste. 200
San Francisco, CA 94111

ISBN-13: 978-0615876627
ISBN-10: 0615876625

Printed in the United States of America
First Edition

This book points out what is possible if we step outside of what we know, and recognize and embrace our capacity to bring forth an entirely new possibility for living—not because it is better, but simply because that is what human beings can do.

Stimulating Risk Is Inseparable from Living

Nothing is so reckless as waiting for certainty—that's a game we are sure to lose. Anyone who runs a business, chooses a mate, or just drives down the street knows there's a risk. When the possibility of power, effectiveness, and freedom arises, we often find ourselves asking "what if the ball actually goes over the fence…. What if it doesn't?" The question of whether something will happen or not is irrelevant to the phenomenon of possibility. There is no certainty as an inevitability, or predictability of the outcome—*we* are the ones *saying* something is possible. Real power occurs when we know we have something to *say* about the way things are—that we have access to the state of affairs beyond just reporting.

Creating possibility is risky business. Creation is a great risk, a kind of ultimate risk—the willingness to take a stand with no evidence. It's hard to provide evidence, or make any real argument for a place where life can show up as a creation, but it is in that domain that the full world available to us in being human can be explored and lived. We cheat ourselves when we try to reduce the risk. What's critical, what makes a difference, is to be left with a choice. And to be left with a choice means to be left fully at risk. Stimulating those risks is inseparable from living.

What Forwards and What Constrains

How we describe, label, hold things, think things—it's within those frameworks that our lives unfold. There are no "facts" that limit possibility, there are only "conversations" that limit and constrain, or those that create and forward, what's possible.

The "glass-half-empty" folks lean toward the idea that something's wrong, something's not there, something's missing-as in problematic. The "half-full" folks are attending to what's actually in the glass-as in what could be brought to the party-as in "missing as a possibility."

If we're going to create a possibility, it's a matter of choosing, a matter of saying, and that's the whole deal. It's about discovering what's possible in being human beyond the places where, unknowingly or knowingly, we might restrict or limit ourselves.

When we create "something missing as a possibility," we set a point of choice, a point of commitment—things show up as openings for action.

Encountering "Nothing" as a Freedom

"Where would something happen if there wasn't nothing? There could be no motion between bodies, no music minus silence, no rhythm without pause, no meaning without space between words, no emptiness out of which new thoughts, new works, might arise. We couldn't calculate, compose, or create without nothing."[1]

The idea of nothing can sometimes be difficult, because we're pretty much wired to perceive experiences, things, concepts as meaningful. The notion of "nothing" can seem antithetical to common-sense views held in our culture. We live in a world where meaning is attached to almost everything, but not as if we were the ones who assigned the meaning. The meanings we live inside of, and hold as fundamental, define our relationships with the world and give us a sense of who we are. To step outside that structure and encounter nothing as a freedom, we have to pass through and beyond the foreignness of the idea.

The "nothing" that's available for us to experience is not nothing as a negation of self but rather as an opening for our selves, a clearing that leaves us with the full range of possibility that's available to us in being human. Nothing is elusive—while we may get it and then lose it again and again, getting it even once is an experience we never get over. It changes the game. When we are able to access nothing, we are able to create, design, and live with a freedom that's not available when we create from something.

Oh, Those Silly Humans...

(Oh, those silly humans! So desperate for their absolutes!) Sometimes it seems like the only job of the world is to gently (or not so gently) separate us from our deepest assurances...Maybe you, too, were once absolutely sure that you'd found your great love, the perfect financial advisor, or the perfect mentor, meditation, or medication that would—once and for all—never fail you. And then? Slowly, things became not so sure, after all. Such is our slippery toehold on "what's real...." [2]

We construct realities and then forget we were the ones who constructed them. When our relationship with reality has a kind of "is-ness" or "fixed-ness" to it, it limits what's possible and allows only for options like explaining, trying to fix, resisting, or accepting. The answer to the question, what does it mean to be human, gets looked at only through that lens. The movie The Matrix captures it: "Welcome to the desert of the real."

The good news is that "reality" is a phenomenon that arises in language. The world does not speak. Only we do. Knowing that allows us to shake up realities we'd taken for granted. It doesn't get rid of the lens or filters or mindsets per se, but they stop defining who we are. With the unsettling of old realities, we become interested in what *might* be, what we can *imagine*. New worlds, new possibilities open up.

Business Not as Usual

At some point today, you're likely to hear someone utter a cry of defeat: IMPOSSIBLE. You may hear it ricochet through the corridors of a company. You may hear it from a colleague, a family member, or friend. And be careful. Let your guard down and you may hear it from the most damning place of all—yourself. "Impossible" is the early warning sign of giving up. Should you hear this word or any of its offspring—unfeasible, impractical, incompatible, unsolvable, insurmountable—stop everything. And do what ever it takes to eradicate their prefixes.[3]

Every day we are presented with opportunities to live as if it's business as usual or to create something beyond who we've been and what we know. Taking new ground—whether it's in expressing ourselves individually and fully, questioning firmly held assumptions, making the difference we're out to make—requires disrupting our old conversations. The skill of the twenty-first century could be said to be the ability to learn, unlearn, and relearn. Unlearning is required when the conversations we revert to no longer work, or the world has changed so completely that they are now holding us back. There is no right place to begin, and we may not know what to do or how to do it, but the pull is there to move what we see or imagine as possible into action. Beyond business as usual—beyond just showing up and living life day after day—is the ability to choose and create a future we really want and will dare to make happen.

Jupid, Jupiter, Jupidest—The Next, Best, Better Thing

Hundreds of flavors of ice cream, countless selections of movie channels, an infinite choice of mates, our daily round of work and play, our incessant getting and spending—the pull of "more, better, different" is everywhere.

It looks a lot like this: we search around and move around and do things and act and keep expanding and going for more or better or different and sometimes we get kind of stuck. But then we break out and we find a new place in life and we are off again expanding and growing and we keep on doing things and often get more from or better at doing that. And that's what life's like. We might avoid the question "is this it" or "is this all there is" for a while, especially when we don't have enough of what we're after. But after we've got "enough," the odds are we'll visit those questions yet again.

More, better, different is the *language of change*—it's comparative, understood in light of the past. It's about *becoming*. The *language of possibility* originates in the future, not the past. It's about *being*, not becoming. Creating possibility is a stand, a declaration of *who we are* and what we're out to create. It's not taking *what is* and changing it—it's taking what isn't, and having it be. It's about creating an extraordinary life as a place from which to come rather than a place to get—it's about living life as a creative act.

JUPID

JUPITER

JUPIDEST

MOLVIG

The Art of Inventing Ourselves

For most of us, "I" is positional ("you" are there and "I" am here). Does this "I" presume a substantial entity located inside our bodies, our minds, our families, job titles, online profiles, bank accounts—those trappings that help us maintain the meanings that we have up 'til now considered ourselves to be?

How we *arrive* at this identity is mostly inadvertent. Essentially it is built from a series of decisions we made in response to what we felt or saw (consciously or not) as failures to do or be something. When these "apparent" failures arose, we made decisions about how to compensate, respond, and accommodate to them. The degree to which who we are today is filtered by those early decisions goes unrecognized. Whether it is one or 10 or even 40 years later, we still hold on to that with which we've identified, obscuring access to ourselves and leaving us no powerful way to be. But stepping outside of our identity isn't so easy—it's all we know of ourselves.

The idea that another whole idea of self is available can be disconcerting. In setting aside those things that gave us an "identity" we "become aware that this so-called self is as arbitrary as our name. It's like standing over an abyss, recognizing that 'I,' as we know it is not an absolute."[4] But it is here, with this recognition, where transformation occurs—where we can invent ourselves as we go along. This revealing of our selves to ourselves occurs in a profound way that can alter the very possibility of what it means to be human.

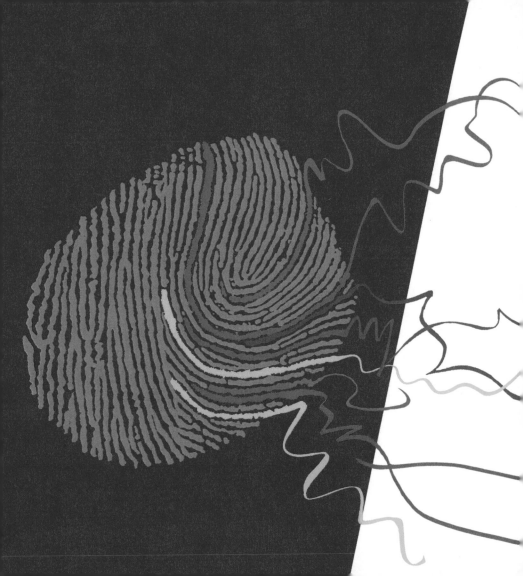

A Portal to the Domain of Possibility

Something happens. Immediately, we assign meaning, categorize importance, draw conclusions, identify action to be taken, form opinions that linger. This collapse between what happened and the meanings we assign takes place so instantaneously that we forget that what happened and how we hold it were two independent and totally separate occurrences. One reinforces the other, and a "vicious circle" gets set in motion. What's disempowering is that in that collapse, realities unwittingly get set.

We then see our lives and ourselves in terms of those realities ("truths," really) and we map our behavior and future experiences onto those "truths." And it's from here that we create the stuff and story of our lives–with a few basic themes playing themselves out over and over. We can spice up or water down our stories, tell the long or short version, add drama or subtlety, but regardless of how clever we are, or what new or different set of circumstances we put into the vicious circle, what we get out of it is only more of the same.

Knowing our stories are an interpretation, and that that's not who we are, produces a portal to a third domain. Possibility exists in this third domain. Possibility moves things around until our experience and our circumstances are a match for what we're out to create. Distinguishing that is transformational. It shifts the horizon of what's possible.

...something happens

THE COLLAPSE
(realities get set)

...meanings get assigned

Fulfilling Your Own Genius

Imagine a great artist like Mozart before the possibility of piano. Or if Hitchcock had lived before the technology of film. Or Van Gogh before oil paints. Undoubtedly those giants would have done their best with whatever they had—perhaps Beethoven on drums, Hitchcock with puppets.

They were able to realize their true genius by finding a perfect match with their tools—tools that are possibilities.[5]

We, too, have the tools in our hands—tools that are a match for what we are out to create, tools for creating possibility...for living lives of our own design, for making the difference we're out to make, for fulfilling our own genius.

When Power and Freedom Emerge

When we're out to create a breakthrough, step outside any constraints of our circumstances, and stand for something we don't know how to achieve, we don't reference what we're out to create against who we'd been or what has been done in the past, what's predictable or expected, but rather against what's possible. It requires leaving behind old conversations like: "circumstances are a way because…" and its corollary "I am powerless because…" When we can see stops, constraints, breakdowns as an *invention*, a *saying*, a *making up*, that affords us a larger opening–power and freedom have room to emerge. Having power, success, and freedom is a lot more risky than having no power. It seems as if an automatic, built-in lock on "no power" comes into play. What if things go wrong? What if they work brilliantly?

Within a few months of Václav Havel's ascension as president of Czechoslovakia, when the euphoria of the Velvet Revolution began to fade, Havel said that he felt "strangely paralyzed." "At the very deepest core of this feeling there was, ultimately, a sensation of the absurd: what Sisyphus might have felt if one fine day his boulder stopped, rested on the hilltop, and failed to roll back down. It was the sensation of a Sisyphus mentally unprepared for the possibility that his efforts might in fact succeed, a Sisyphus whose life had lost its old purpose."[6] In creating possibility, we get to know what's possible in being human.

Possibility—More Like Dancing than Stepping

Most of us can ride a bicycle, but no one actually knows *how* it is done. Not even engineers or bicycle manufacturers know the "formula" for balancing—there's no "right" method of counteracting the tendency to fall by turning the handlebars. Tutorials, diagrams, explanation don't do the trick. We have to *discover* balance, distinguish balance from a largely undifferentiated background and when we do, it establishes a new realm of possibility.

Because we listen a lot of the time for formulas, we often think of possibility like there is a formula. From formulas, we learn what works; how best to navigate; what knowledge to apply, when, where, and how. A lot gets accomplished by formula—but not possibility. Possibility does not play out in a clear-cut way (black/white, correct/incorrect, true/false). When we create a realm of possibility, it will exist in time and place. When it manifests, it will manifest in time and place, and will move in the direction of some formula—so it is worth paying attention to this business about formula. But we can disempower ourselves if we get "stuck" there.

When a new realm of possibility gets created (along with the accompanying freedom to be and act within that realm) it has a vastly different impact on the quality of our lives than those things that live as a formula. In this new space we're dealing with the same things, but they occur in a new way because we're dealing with them in a new paradigm. Everything that was powerful in the formula is still there, still available—but it looks like dancing instead of stepping.

Peace of Mind—Giving Up the Notion that "Something's Wrong Here"

At some point, early on in life, stuff happens that doesn't quite work out how we think it should. In those moments we come to believe that "there's something wrong here." Our successes, relationships, personality, and accomplishments then get assembled to adapt to that sense of things. We put together ways of being that work for us, that achieve results, provide pleasure, and make us the people we are today. The joy, pleasure, and satisfaction that we experience obscure the notion that something's not quite right. Peace of mind (power and fulfillment, too) requires the intersection with, and recognition of, the way we've constructed ourselves.

Peace of mind comes from giving up the notion that "something's wrong here." Giving that up is like having the ability to dance–like the extraordinary performance of a matador or an aikido master–with what's so and with what comes at us vs. how we thought or hoped it would go. It leaves us with a sense of ease, a congruence with ourselves, a feeling of being at home–where we are not constrained by "shoulds" or "watch outs," but free to act, free to move, free to be fully ourselves.

...d is genera[l]

and contentment.

Peace of mind \pés...

refers to a state of be[ing]

mentally and spiritual[ly]

peace, with enough k[nowledge]

and understanding to [be]

strong in the face of [st]-

[st]ress. Being "at [peace]" [is consi]dered b...

Breakdowns—The Good, the Bad, and the Opening for Action

Breakdowns and upsets are pretty much a double-sided affair. On the inside of the box, they're "inevitable," on the outside of the box they "shouldn't be." That mix sets the stage for a crazy-making dynamic right from the start. (Plus, it invites a familiar overlay—the not very empowering litany of "...what's wrong with them, me, it?") When our attention is primarily directed to how wrong things are, we lose our power to act effectively. What's worth noting is: There's no such thing as a breakdown without a commitment in the background. Commitments express themselves in agreements and expectations (declared and/or undeclared). If we take out the commitment and only have "what is," there are no breakdowns—breakdowns are constituted by commitment. If we look at what the commitment is in the background (that makes what happened in the foreground a breakdown) we'd have a very different kind of power.

Effective people invent possibilities to which they're committed and deal with breakdowns as they come up. They have an awesome commitment to completing the breakdown. There's no hint of good/bad, "should or shouldn't be," just that "there are breakdowns" as an inevitable and invited component of any commitment. Seeing and engaging with breakdowns in this way alters the dynamic from one we might experience as thwarting or frustrating, to an occurrence that's an invention, a making up, something to be embraced and valued—an opportunity to move things forward, to provide what's missing, to be a powerful opening for action.

Creative Acts—The Edge of Freedom

We commonly think of freedom as "freedom from," "freedom of," or "freedom to" do or be something, or as the ability to define alternatives and select among them. "But freedom far exceeds anything on that spectrum–it's being able to redefine ourselves and reality at large, generating whole new sets of possibilities. History is punctuated by such redefinitions–creative acts that open new worlds. In this sense, we can call creative acts the edge of freedom–the faculty by which, down through history, we have redefined our world and ourselves."[7]

Freedom is not like other phenomena. It's closer to "being" than it is to some "thing." It has nothing to do with options. It requires dimensionality–if we try to move freedom through a world of limited possibility, it can never show up as itself, it's always distorted as something else. Freedom doesn't live in a temporality like past, present, and future–it doesn't stop, in the same way that "number" doesn't stop giving numbers or that art is not repeating, in a new way, the past. There's nothing pulling one way or the other, there is just this awesome freedom. Freedom is about choosing–it's about the profoundly human ability to create.

CREATIVE
ACTS:
THE
DGE

FREEDOM

A fundamental principle of Landmark's work is that people and the communities and organizations with which they are engaged have the possibility of not only success, but also fulfillment and greatness. It is to this possibility that Landmark and its work are committed.

www.landmarkworldwide.com

Endnotes

1. Adapted from Joan Konner, *You Don't Have to Be Buddhist to Know Nothing* (Promethius Books, 2009).

2. Adapted from Elizabeth Gilbert, *What Elizabeth Gilbert Knows for Sure About Certainty*, O Magazine (November 2008).

3. Adapted with permission. ©Bull HN Information Systems, Inc.

4. Adapted from Colin Wilson, *The Mind Parasites* (Oneiric Press, 1990).

5. Kevin Kelly, *The Technium and the 7th Kingdom of Life,* Edge: The Third Culture (19 July 2007).

6. Adapted from David Remnick, *Exit Havel,* The New Yorker (17 February 2003).

7. Robert Grudin, *The Grace of Great Things* (Mariner Books, 1990).

Made in the USA
Columbia, SC
21 July 2017